DECLARE
YOUR
DESTINY

Unleash the Power
of Spoken Words

By John Marshall

Declare Your Destiny – Unleash the Power of Spoken Words

By John Marshall

ISBN 0-9740693-1-0

Text layout and design by Cathleen Kwas, CLicK Services, Lake Mary Florida.

DEDICATION

I dedicate this book to my father, Mr. Cleveland Marshall, (1906-1998). Always the tone and text of his speech indicated the power of words. What he said he meant, and meant to happen. Rarely, did we hesitate to do what he said when he said to do it. And never did we decide to not do what he said to do when he said to do it. Long before I realized the spiritual concept of the power of words, I was practicing it at home. For daddy demanded that we honor and obey the words of our mother just as we did his. Indeed, he is my hero.

Daddy was the son of a former slave (my grandfather was sixteen years old when the president signed the Emancipation Proclamation). Growing up sharecropping in Mississippi taught him many valuable principles and lessons, which he instilled in me.

Daddy believed that God would come to the rescue of those who treated others fairly. Therefore, he always spoke up for those whom he believed were being wronged.

Daddy believed that God would somehow provide the information that you needed by the time you needed it. Therefore, he never hesitated to give what he believed to be was appropriate advice.

Daddy always kept his word, for his word was his bond and he insisted on your word being your bond. As I enjoy the pleasure and endure the pain of ministry, daily I depend upon the character principles of my daddy to enable me to succeed.

Even as I write the words of this dedication, I cannot resist the tears of thankfulness as I appreciate a father's training that was well done. Indeed my daddy is my hero.

TABLE OF CONTENTS

DECLARE YOUR DESTINY – UNLEASH THE POWER OF SPOKEN WORDS

INTRODUCTION

What are the things you want for your life? None of us have ever prayed and asked to be cursed, ill treated or afflicted in anyway. Most of us, when we make our holiday wish list hope that we'll get the things we've requested from those we've asked. Why? Is it because we've spoken goodness into their heart by the words we've said to them? Maybe you feel that you'll not get the things you wanted because you've not only cursed yourself by the words of your mouth, but you "*cursed*" them as well by the callousness of your tongue.

We have trained or can train every kind of animal or bird that lives and every kind of reptile and fish, but no human being can tame the tongue. It is always ready to pour out its deadly poison. Sometimes it praises our Heavenly Father, and sometimes it breaks out into curses against men who are made like God. And so blessings and cursing come pouring out of the same mouth. It is not right.

(James 3:7-10, paraphrased**)**

If we know that it's not right, and that within our own limited power we cannot tame our tongue, then what are we to do?

But the wisdom that comes from heaven is first of all pure and full of quiet gentleness. Then it is peaceable, loving and courteous. It allows discussion and is <u>willing to yield</u> to others; it is full of mercy and good deeds. It is wholehearted, straightforward, and sincere. And those who are peacemakers will plant seed of peace and reap a harvest of goodness.

(James 17-18, paraphrased**)**

Asking for wisdom is one of the first steps to gaining control over what we speak into our lives and into the lives of others.

I pray that after reading this book, you will come to have what you say you want to have by using your tongue to speak the righteousness of God.

CHAPTER ONE

DIVINE PROOF
OF THE POWER
OF WORDS...

Divine Proof of the Power of Words...

What is the most powerful member of your body? Is it your eyes, fingers, legs, toes, thumbs, ears or heart?

> *For this reason it is by faith, in order that it may be in accordance with grace, so that the promise will be guaranteed to all the descendants, not only to those who are of the Law, but also to those who are of the faith of Abraham, who is the father of us all, (as it is written, "A FATHER OF MANY NATIONS HAVE I MADE YOU") in the presence of Him whom*

he believed, even God, who gives life to the dead and calls into being that which does not exist.

(Romans 4:16-17)

God calls it into being by the power of His word. He always said before He did. He said it first and then it happened. He never did what He had not already said and He never did more than He said. Speaking things into existence is His mode of operation.

At times He did not do all that He said; but there were never times when He did not say all that He did. From the power of the words He spoke, that which exists came into its existence.

Your spoken words are a most powerful force within the universe. They exert powerful influence within your circle. But even beyond your known circle of influence, when you speak, you unleash a very powerful force throughout the entire universe.

At Creation God Said Before He Did

God spoke the non-living elements into existence. *"Then God said, 'Let there be light'; and there was light"* **(Genesis 1:3)**. When did light come into existence? Light came into existence, *only*, after God spoke it into existence.

Then God said, "Let there be an expanse in the midst of the waters, and let it separate the waters from the waters." God made the expanse, and separated the waters which were below the expanse from the waters which were above the expanse; and it was so. God called the expanse heaven. And there was evening and there was morning, a second day. Then God said, "Let the waters below the heavens be gathered into one place, and let the dry land appear"; and it was so. God called the dry land earth, and the gathering of the waters He called seas; and God saw that it was good.

(Genesis 1:6-10)

When did the waters separate? When did the waters gather in one place? They separated and gathered only after God spoke. God said before He did. The power of His word brought reality to pass. That which He said about the non-living elements of the universe came to pass.

God spoke the living of creation into existence. Like the non-living elements of creation, God's word brought forth the living of creation:

Then God said, "Let the earth sprout vegetation, plants yielding seed, and fruit trees on the earth bearing fruit after their kind with seed in them"; and it was so. The earth brought forth vegetation, plants yielding seed after their kind, and trees bearing fruit with seed in them, after their kind; and God saw that it was good.

(Genesis 1:11-12)

Then God said, "Let the waters teem with swarms of living creatures, and let birds fly above the earth in the open expanse of the heavens." God created the great monsters and every living creature that moves, with which the waters swarmed after their kind, and every winged bird after its kind; and God saw that it was good.

(Genesis 1:20-21)

Then God said, "Let the earth bring forth living creatures after their kind: cattle and creeping things and beasts of the earth after their kind"; and it was so. God made the beasts of the earth after their kind, and the cattle after their kind and *everything that creeps on the ground after its kind; and God saw that it was good.*

(Genesis 1:24-25)

Then God said, "Let Us make man in Our image according to Our likeness; and let them rule over the fish of the sea and over the birds of the sky and over the cattle and over all the earth, and over every creeping thing that creeps on the earth." God created man in His own image, in the image of God He created him; male and female He created them.

(Genesis 1:26-27)

Time and time again, God said before it came to pass. What came to pass had already been said.

After Creation God Said Before He Did

At creation, God said before He did. After creation God continued to say before He did.

Then the Lord God said, "It is not good for the man to be alone; I will make him a helper suitable for him."

(Genesis 2:18)

God said it before He did it:

Then God said to Noah, "The end of all flesh has come before Me; for the earth is filled with violence because of them; and behold, I am about to destroy them with the earth. Make for yourselves an ark of gopher wood; you shall make the ark with rooms, and shall cover it inside and out with pitch"...Thus Noah did; according to all that God had commanded him so he did.

(Genesis 6:13-22)

God said it and then He did it:

"Come, let Us go down and there confuse their language, so that they will not understand one another's speech." So the Lord scattered them abroad from there over the face of the whole earth; and they stopped building the city. Therefore its name was called Babel, because there the Lord confused the language of the whole *earth; and from there the Lord scattered them abroad over the face of the whole earth."*

(Genesis 11:7-9)

Jesus Demonstrated the Power of the Spoken Word

And when Jesus entered Capernaum, a centurion came to Him, imploring Him, and saying, "Lord my servant is lying paralyzed at home, fearfully tormented." Jesus said to him, "I will come and heal him."

(Matthew 8:5-7)

Jesus said that He would come and heal the centurion's servant. Therefore, the centurion expected Jesus to do what He had said. Will Jesus make good on His promise?

But the centurion said, "Lord I am not worthy for you to come under my roof, but just say the word, and my servant will be healed."

(Matthew 8:8)

The centurion encouraged Jesus not to come. He knew that the power to heal was not in the power of the physical presence of Jesus but in the power of the spoken word of Jesus. He believed that all Jesus needed to do was to say it and it would happen. The centurion said:

> *"For I also am a man under authority, with soldiers under me; and I say to one, 'Go!' and he goes, and to another, 'Come!' and he comes, and to my slave, 'Do this! and he does it.'"*
> **(Matthew 8:9)**

The centurion was likely a Gentile. But faith in the power of the spoken word pleased our Lord:

> *"Now when Jesus heard this, He marveled and said to those who were following, 'Truly I say to you, I have not found such great faith with anyone in Israel'...And Jesus said to the centurion, 'Go; it shall be done for you as you have believed. And the servant was healed that very moment"*
> **(Matthew 8:10,13).**

What did the he centurion believe? He believed that it could be done with the spoken word. Jesus said that because the centurion believed that his servant could be healed with the spoken word it would be done with the spoken word. The servant was healed at that very hour. Jesus demonstrated that there was power in the spoken word.

Jesus Told of the Power of the Spoken Word

> *The good man brings out of his good treasure what is good; and the evil man brings out of his evil treasure what is evil. But I tell you that every careless word that people speak, they shall give accounting for it in the day of judgment. For by your words you will be justified, and by your words you will be condemned.*
>
> **(Matthew 12:35-37)**

Every word—none excluded—that you speak is a word of power and influence. Your words have the power to justify or condemn you. Do you speak justifying words or do you speak condemning words?

Your tongue speaks words that are from

your heart. Therefore, what you say is who you are. If you are constantly speaking darkness, that's what you are, a person in darkness.

> *Either make the tree good and its fruit good, or make the tree bad and its fruit bad; for the tree is known by its fruit. You brood of vipers, how can you, being evil, speak what is good? For the mouth speaks out of that which fills the heart.*
>
> **(Matthew 12:33-34)**

Jesus made this statement as a prelude to verses 35-37. He taught that if you were good you would speak good, but if you were bad, you would speak bad. Let's state these same truths in reverse. If you speak good it is because you are good. If you speak bad it is because you are bad.

Time and time again Jesus underscored that what you say comes from your heart. But some will say, *"I am just saying what they told me."*

Every Monday two brown trucks come by my house. One of those brown trucks stops in front of my house and the men pick up whatever I have set at the curb. This is the garbage truck.

Another brown truck also comes by my house. Sometimes it stops right in front of my house. But the men never pick up the garbage. Even if I insisted, he will not take the garbage. He refuses to accept it. This is the UPS truck.

The UPS driver is not a garbage collector. Therefore, he doesn't behave like one. Garbage collecting is not his profession, and picking up garbage is not his purpose.

Sometimes the UPS truck arrives at my house before the garbage truck gets there. Yet, the driver is smart enough to leave the garbage alone. If he started picking up garbage, he would be judged by the garbage he picks up. If he does start picking up garbage, he would lose his job with UPS. He would be condemned for hauling that which he is not supposed to haul.

Unless you desire to be a garbage collector, do not collect the garbage of others. Unless you want to be garbage, when you are in the midst of garbage, don't pick up garbage and pass it along.

There is nothing wrong with being a garbage collector. It is better to pick up garbage and earn an honest, decent living than to stand around with some wicked scheme trying to cheat people out of their money. If garbage collecting is your job, dress for job and pick up garbage with a smile. But, do not complain when you smell like the residue of garbage when the day is over.

The things that come out of the mouth come from the heart. Garbage will not come out of your mouth unless first you have allowed garbage to be put into your heart. *"The good man out of the good treasure of his heart brings forth what is good; and the evil man out of the evil treasure brings forth what is evil; for his mouth speaks from that which fills his heart"* **(Luke 6:45)**.

Your mouth speaks that which fills the heart. Jesus didn't say that the mouth speaks only what is in the heart, but rather that which <u>fills</u> the heart.

Even your worship (singing) flows from that which fills your heart. Your singing should come from the overflow of the word of God within your heart. *"Let the word of Christ richly dwell within you, with all wisdom teaching and admonishing one another with psalms and hymns and spiritual songs, singing with thankfulness in your hearts to God"* **(Colossians 3:16)**.

God desires to engrave the word into your heart. He wants to put it there permanently. To "dwell" means to take up residence and live there. The word of God is not intended to be just a weekend guest, but a permanent resident. Through His Spirit, God engraves His word into your heart. When He has engraved His word in abundance within your heart, you sing.

Your tongue speaks the potentiality of your heart into the reality of your life. That which is potential in your heart, becomes real in your life with the speaking of your tongue.

Whatever you say becomes a powerful spiritual force within your life. Whenever you speak, you always create repercussions within your life. If you say something healthy about yourself you send healthy repercussions throughout your life. But if you say something that's unhealthy about yourself you send unhealthy repercussions throughout your life.

The truth is really very simple: Garbage in garbage out. Junk in junk out. Therefore, prayerfully and carefully choose your words.

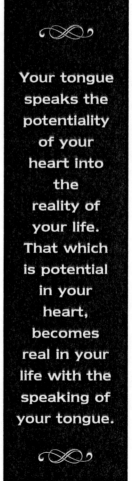

Your tongue speaks the potentiality of your heart into the reality of your life. That which is potential in your heart, becomes real in your life with the speaking of your tongue.

DECLARE YOUR DESTINY - UNLEASH THE POWER OF SPOKEN WORDS

Father let my spoken words be of wisdom, like an ever-flowing stream of health. Let my words heal the hearer and reward my soul.

2

CHAPTER TWO

SPOKEN WORDS CAN CREATE A CURSE WITHIN YOUR LIFE

B SPOKEN WORDS CAN CREATE A CURSE WITHIN YOUR LIFE

But no one can tame the tongue; it is a restless evil and full of deadly poison. With it we bless our Lord and Father, and with it we curse men, who have been made in the likeness of God; from the same mouth come both blessing and cursing.

(James 3:8-10)

No one can tame the tongue. It is a restless evil and full of deadly poison. With your tongue you curse men.

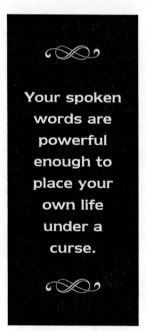

Your spoken words are powerful enough to place your own life under a curse.

Your spoken words are very powerful, and can be a destructive force in the universe. Your words have the power to destroy. In fact, your spoken words are powerful enough to place your own life under a curse.

What is a curse? A curse is a divine sentence of punishment. A curse lines up the universal forces in opposition to your well-being.

Jesus entered Jerusalem and came into the temple; and after looking around at everything, He left for Bethany with the twelve, since it was already late. On the next day, when they had left Bethany, He became hungry. Seeing at a distance a fig tree in leaf, He went to see if perhaps He would find anything on it; and when He came to it, He found nothing but leaves, for it was not the season for figs. He said to it, "May no one ever eat fruit from you again!" And His disciples were listening... When evening came, they would go out of the city. As they were passing by in the morning, they saw the fig tree withered from the roots up. Being reminded, Peter said to Him, "Rabbi, look, the fig tree which you cursed has withered."

(Mark 11:11-21)

The fig tree was cursed by the mighty power of spoken words. Using the power of his spoken word, Jesus cursed the fig tree. His spoken words took the very life out of the tree and it withered from the root in one day.

Your tongue charts the course of your life. Your life will go in the direction that your tongue leads it.

Let not many of you become teachers, my brethren, knowing that as such we will incur a stricter judgment. For we all stumble in many ways. If anyone does not stumble in what he says, he is a perfect man, able to bridle the whole body as well. Now if we put the bits into the horses' mouths so that they will obey us, we direct their entire body as well. Look at the ships also, though they are so great and are driven by strong winds, are still directed by a very small rudder wherever the inclination of the pilot desires. So also the tongue is a small part of the body, and yet it boasts of great things.

See how great a forest is set aflame by such a small fire! And the tongue is a fire, the very world of iniquity; the tongue is set among our members as that which defiles the entire body, and sets on fire the course of our life, and is set on fire by hell. For every species of beasts and birds, of reptiles and creatures of the sea, is tamed and has been tamed by the human race. But no one can tame the tongue; it is a restless evil and full of deadly poison. With it we bless our Lord and Father, and with it we curse men, who have been made in the likeness of God; from the same mouth come both blessing and cursing. My brethren, these things ought not to be this way.

(James 3:1-10)

Why is your life so messed up? Your life is messed up because you have been following your tongue and it's been leading you in the wrong direction. Therefore, you must change the course of your tongue.

From where do cursings come? They come from your tongue.

> *A worthless man digs up evil, while his words are as a scorching fire.*
>
> *A man of violence entices his neighbor and leads him in a way that is not good.*
>
> *He who winks his eyes does so to devise perverse things; he who compresses his lips brings evil to pass.*
>
> **(Proverbs 16:27,29,30)**

> *A fool's lips bring strife and his mouth calls for blows.*
>
> *A fool's mouth is his ruin, and his lips are the snare of his soul.*
>
> **(Proverbs 18:6-7)**

> *The words of a whisperer are like dainty morsels, and they go down into the innermost parts of the body.*
>
> **(Proverbs 18:8)**

> *The words of a whisperer are like dainty morsels and they go down into the innermost parts of the body.*

Like an earthen vessel overlaid with silver dross are burning lips and a wicked heart.

He who hates disguises it with his lips, but he lays up deceit in his heart.

(Proverbs 26:22-25)

Where do words go? They go down into the body, into the spirit of the person. Hearing and speaking words is similar to eating tasty food. Speaking idle words is like standing around eating finger food. You must be very careful or you will indulge in much more than you intended.

Death is in the power of the tongue (Proverbs 18:21). Because of this truth, you have the ability to speak death into your own life. You will eat the fruit of the words that you speak.

"He who guards his mouth and his tongue, guards his soul from troubles" **(Proverbs 21:23).** What is the opposite? The person who does not guard his mouth and his tongue makes his soul vulnerable for trouble. When you aren't guarding your mouth, you open yourself up for a lot of trouble.

For the lack of wood the fire goes out, and where there is no whisperer, contention quiets down.

Like charcoal to hot embers and wood to fire, so is a contentious man to kindle strife.

(Proverbs 26:20-21)

The fire goes out when the wood is consumed. Likewise, contention ends when busybodies and gossips have no news to tell.

Contentious people always infect others. Contentious seniors have created contentious juniors waiting for the seniors to die so they can rise to prominence. Therefore, the contentiousness continues even after the first generation of contentious people dies.

A lying tongue hates those it crushes, and a flattering mouth works ruin.

(Proverbs 26:28).

Your words can curse the circumstances of your life. Be careful what you say. Do not curse yourself by saying, *"I will probably fail."* or *"My children will probably abandon me when I am old."* or *"I know that will not work."*

For years, comedian Redd Foxx would clutch his chest and say, *"I'm having the big one!"* but he was just kidding. However, when he really was "having the big one" people thought he was just kidding, and he died.

You can set in motion death by what you say because there is power in the tongue. Therefore, you must eliminate destructive words from your conversation.

"For what I fear comes upon me, and what I dread befalls me" **(Job 3:25).** What Job feared is just what happened to him.

At the judgment, God will not play the video of your life. He will play the audio instead. Why? Because, what you have said is what you are.

With your tongue uttering prayers to God, you can accomplish things in Africa without ever leaving America. However, with your hands you have to go to Africa to get things done. Your tongue is a very powerful member of your body.

Your words cause spiritual repercussions. That's the way God designed it. If you're sitting in a boat on peaceful waters you'll see that a dropped rock causes waves (repercussions). This is a simple law of physics: For every action there is an equal and opposite reaction.

Your spoken words can be a powerfully destructive force or they can be a powerful constructive force. Whether your words will destroy or whether they will construct; whether they will build up or will tear down, it's up to YOU. You are responsible for what your words will do.

God grant me the opportunity to empty my heart of the evil therein so that I will never again speak evil of myself or of anyone else. God, I know that you love me and willingly forgive. Improve the quality of my life.

3

SPOKEN WORDS CAN CREATE A BLESSING WITHIN YOUR LIFE

B

SPOKEN WORDS CAN CREATE A BLESSING WITHIN YOUR LIFE

But no one can tame the tongue; it is a restless evil and full of deadly poison. With it we bless our Lord and Father, and with it we curse men, who have been made in the likeness of God.

(James 3:8-9)

No one can tame the tongue. Yet, it can be channeled productively. With your tongue you bless the Lord.

Your spoken words are a very powerful constructive force within the universe. Your words have the power to create. Your spoken words are powerful enough to place your own life under a blessing.

What is a blessing? What does it mean to be blessed? To be blessed is to be positioned for prosperity. To be positioned for prosperity is to have people and circumstances synchronized and favorably aligned for your benefit.

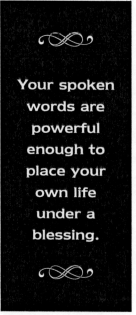

Your spoken words are powerful enough to place your own life under a blessing.

For example, you need a job. Employee R calls in to company A at 7:45 am speaks with personnel manager M and resigns immediately. At 7:55 am, you apply for a job at company A. You are immediately hired by personnel manger M. In this event, circumstances and people are aligned favorably for you. Those who showed up looking for a job at 10:00 am failed to have circumstances favorably aligned for them. Those who applied for a job a day earlier when the company was not in need of employees also failed to have circumstances favorably aligned for them. They were not blessed in this endeavor.

After these things there was a feast of the Jews, and Jesus went up to Jerusalem.

Now there is in Jerusalem by the sheep gate a pool, which is called in Hebrew Bethesda, having five porticoes. In these lay a multitude of those who were sick, blind, lame, and withered, [waiting for the moving of the waters; for an angel of the Lord went down at certain seasons into the pool and stirred up the water; whoever then first, after the stirring up of the water, stepped in was made well from whatever disease with which he was afflicted.] A man was there who had been ill for thirty-eight years. When Jesus saw him lying there, and knew that he had already been a long time in that condition, He said to him, "Do you wish to get well?" The sick man answered Him, "Sir, I have no man to put me into the pool when the water is stirred up, but while I am coming, another steps down before me." Jesus said to him, "Get up, pick up your pallet and walk." Immediately the man became well, and picked up his pallet and began to walk.

Now it was the Sabbath on that day.

(John 5:1-10)

This story illustrates the synchronization of what a blessing really is. When the angel would come to trouble the waters, this man had no one to help him in. When someone was there to help him, the angel did not appear. For thirty-eight years this poor man missed being blessed. Why? People and circumstances were never synchronized favorably for him. You can be in the presence of God but miss being blessed.

Prosperity Is More Than Money

Prosperity is not just something economical. Prosperity is the sum total health of your mental, spiritual, physical, emotional, and psychological economy—all of the dimensions that go into helping you to be a total healthy individual. If you have half the money in the world and your mental, spiritual, physical, emotional, and/or psychological health is ill you have a grave problem.

Now the Lord said to Abram:
"Go forth from your country,
And from your relatives And from

your father's house, To the land which I will show you; And I will make you a great nation, And I will bless you, And make your name great; And so you shall be a blessing; And I will bless those who bless you, And the one who curses you I will curse. And in you all the families of the earth will be blessed."

(Genesis 12:1-3)

God promised to align favorable circumstances and people for Abram. Regardless of your geographical location God possesses the power to favorably align circumstances for you.

The tongue of the righteous is as choice silver. The heart of the wicked is worth little.

The lips of the righteous feed many, but fools die for lack of understanding.

(Proverbs 10:20-21)

The lips of the righteous bring forth what is acceptable but the mouth of the wicked brings what is perverted.

(Proverbs 10:32)

A man will be satisfied with good by the fruit of his words...

(Proverbs 12:14)

What is the fruit of your words? Satisfaction! You will be satisfied with good by the fruit of your word! What you do will return to you.

There is one who speaks rashly like the thrust of a sword, but the tongue of the wise brings healing.

(Proverbs 12:18)

The writer of Proverbs is describing a scenario where there has already been a wound. Something has happened that has created a wound, but the power in the tongue brings forth healing.

Why do people fight? Often it's not because of what happened but because of what was said. If someone were to step on your toe, you would forgive them. But if they said, *"Move your foot out of the way!"* a fight begins. Why? Because of what they said.

The Tongue Is Sharp Like A Sword

When small child falls and cuts their knee, a mother's soothing words, even while the blood is still oozing and the wound still hurts, creates a *"just fine"* emotional healing in the little one. However, if the child falls and harsh words like, *"get up! Stop your crying and act like a grownup."* created an *"I am not just fine"* emotional wound within the child. Then, instead of just one scraped knee, two wounds must be healed.

When you encounter someone who has been wounded, your words can create a healing atmosphere. When you encounter a situation where health has vanished away, are you helpful or harmful? Your words can bring forth a healing.

> *A soothing tongue is a tree of life,*
> *but perversion in it crushes the*
> *spirit.*
> **(Proverbs 15:4)**

A tree keeps on giving fruit! What you say can continue to bring forth life and continue to bring forth health—it's up to you and you will decide.

When you are feeling down, there are certain people that you want to talk to and other people you want to avoid. Some will say things that help you feel better, while others say things that make you feel worse.

Examine yourself. Are situations better after you speak or are they worse? A soothing tongue is a tree of life, but perversion in it crushes the spirit. See, what you say can discourage. Your words can be devastating, and can sap the strength and momentum out of a person. Therefore, do you speak life and energy into circumstances, or do you use your words to be destructive?

> *With the fruit of a man's mouth his stomach will be satisfied; He will be satisfied with the product of his lips.*
> *Death and life are in the power of the tongue, and those who love it will eat its fruit.*
> **(Proverbs 18:20-21)**

> *By the blessing [words] of the upright, a city is exalted, but by the mouth of the wicked it is torn down.*
> **(Proverbs 11:11)**

You are responsible to choose and select words that are healthy and wholesome. It's very likely you are where you are today because of the things you have been saying about yourself.

What do you say about your life? Do you speak healthy, positive things? I know what happens when you begin to talk like that, people will think it's just wishful thinking and they begin to feel uncomfortable.

However, you can badger yourself and nobody cares! You can walk into room filled with people and declare, *"I'm ugly."* You can even say, *"My mother and father are ugly and I have always known that I would really be an ugly child; even my brothers and sisters are ugly."*

Guess what? No one will get upset. No one will disagree. Few people care what you say about yourself as long as it is negative. Some may even agree with you: *"Yes I thought so too."* From others you may receive a little sympathy if they are persuaded that some truth lies within your statements.

But if you walk in and say, *"I am a good looking person, because my mother and father are good looking people."* Guess what? Very likely, some people will get upset, even if what you say is true!

Why the difference in response from the audience? Our society has sold us a negative bill of goods. The devil has convinced believers to interpret affirmative actions as arrogance of the worst sort.

When you speak words that are positive people tend to feel uncomfortable. You must become accustomed to speaking positive words in spite of resistance from others.

I once heard of a preacher, who when members would say to him *"You preached a good sermon."* would say, *"I know. That's the only kind I preach."* No doubt many would think that he was arrogant, but why can't say the same things about his preaching that others do?

The devil uses reverse psychology. He leads you to believe that it's acceptable to criticize yourself but not to compliment yourself. No principle within Scripture validates this dysfunctional thinking.

The devil has tricked you. Often, he has made you feel that you are arrogant if you say something good about yourself. Therefore, pseudo-humility drives you to degrade yourself with your negative words.

Negative Words Create An Attitude of Worry

What are you doing when you worry? You are paying interest today on tomorrow's troubles. You are paying interest on troubles that just might not happen.

Would you pay interest before receiving the borrowed funds? Certainly not! Why then do you prepay interest on yet to be experienced troubles? Be concerned and be prepared, but don't worry, at least until after it has happened, because it might not happen.

Words Supply The Soul

Your words are the supply sergeants of your soul; it is supplied by what you say. What do you want to supply to your soul? Your words can put you in bondage, or they can liberate you.

Where do you prefer to be? Do you prefer to be in bondage or to enjoy liberation? Your words are powerful enough to create the blessing or the curse in your life that you choose.

Imagine having a flat tire while driving to work tomorrow. Imagine getting out of your car and walking around to look at the flat tire. Now, imagine saying to yourself:

> *This tire is flat. There is probably a nail in the tire. As a matter of fact, I know there is a nail in this tire. I saw those children playing with nails, and one of them left the nail on the driveway that punctured my tire. Because I have a flat tire, I am going to be late getting to work. Then, because I'm late, I will be reprimanded. I feel so bad, I think I'll just sit here and cry for awhile."*

If this were how you responded to the situation, you would see after your eyes dried, that the tire is still flat and you're still going to be late for work!

On the other hand, you could get out of the car and while singing a song think to yourself: *"I have a flat, but I also have a spare tire in the trunk. I'll get the jack out, loosen the lug nuts, take off the flat tire and put the spare tire on quickly. Yes, I'll be late. But the sooner I get the tire changed, the sooner I can get to work."*

In spite of problematic situations, talk solution. Satan wants you to speak negatively rather than positively. So why would you choose to obey him?

A woman endured terrible pain in her back. For years, she went to doctor after doctor to no avail. Eventually, a physician discovered that her left leg was one-fourth of an inch shorter than her right leg, causing her spine to twist out of proper alignment. She obtained a left shoe that boosted her height by one-fourth of an inch, which put her spine back into its proper alignment. Her pain was alleviated.

Often the source of the pain is misdiagnosed. Until you discover that your words have "misaligned your spine" and are what is causing your pain nothing will improve. And very likely, you'll spend absolutely too much time re-stating the problem.

Lord, re-align my consciousness with your presence so that I see and speak into existence Your abundant supply of healthy attitudes.

CHAPTER FOUR

SPOKEN WORDS PROGRAM YOUR LIFE FOR LIFE

Spoken Words Program Your Life For Life

DNA is the genetic code that regulates your life. Likewise, your spoken words are a type of spiritual DNA that regulates much of life. Indeed, you program yourself for life by the words that you speak.

And when I came to you, brethren, I did not come with superiority of speech or of wisdom, proclaiming to you the testimony of God. For I determined to know nothing among you except Jesus Christ, and Him crucified. I was with you in weakness and in fear and in much trembling, and my message and my preaching were not in persuasive words of wisdom, but in demonstration of the Spirit and of power, so that your faith would not rest on the wisdom of men, but on the power of God.

(1 Corinthians 2:1-5)

The preaching of the Apostle Paul was in demonstration of the Spirit and of power. What exactly was the demonstration of the power? The <u>message</u> that he preached was the demonstration of power. He preached so that their faith would not rest on the wisdom of men, but on the power of God.

Their faith rested on the power of God, his preached message. The very message that he preached was the very power of God. Of what did his message consist? His message consisted of words. His spoken words were the very power of God. Spoken words are

> Like your genetic DNA that regulates your biological life, your spoken words are a type of spiritual DNA that regulates your soteriological life.

the power force of God that is active within the universe.

> *For to us God revealed them through the Spirit; for the Spirit searches all things, even the depths of God. For who among men knows the thoughts of a man except the spirit of the man which is in him? Even so the thoughts of God no one knows except the Spirit of God. Now we have received, not the spirit of the world, but the Spirit who is from God, so that we may know the things freely given to us by God.*
> **(1 Corinthians 2:10-12)**

What had the Apostle Paul received? He had received the Spirit of God. Therefore, he argued that God revealed his message through His Spirit. Yes, the Holy Spirit revealed the very words that Paul spoke.

Why did Paul receive the Spirit of God? He received the Spirit of God so that he could know the things freely given by God.

To receive the word of God into your heart is to receive the word of God into your spirit. When you receive the word of God into your spirit, you have the very power of God available to you. The word is power.

> *Now to Him who is able to do far more abundantly beyond all that we ask or think, according to the power that works within us...*
> **(Ephesians 3:20)**

God is able to do more than you can ask or even think to ask, because the power of God exceeds your intellectual capacity. You may wonder how manifests His power beyond your intellectual capacity. He does so according to the power that works within you, which is the engraved word of God. When God engraves His word in your heart, you have the very power force of God working within you.

When repentant hearers of the gospel become baptized, God gives them His Holy Spirit.

> *Peter said to them, "Repent, and each of you be baptized in the name of Jesus Christ for the forgiveness of your sins; and you will receive the gift of the Holy Spirit."*
> **(Acts 2:38)**

> *And we are witnesses of these things; and so is the Holy Spirit, whom God has given to those who obey Him.*
> **(Acts 5:32)**

God is Spirit. He communicates through His spirit to your spirit. He has re-created the spirit of believers so that He can communicate with them. When believers speak from their heart, they activate the very power of God.

Regularly, dynamite travels through your city. Though it carries the potential for destruction, it rests powerless until the fuse is lit. When the fuse it lit, the power of the explosive is unleashed. So it is with the power of God. It rests powerless until its fuse it lit. Your spoken words light the fuse and unleashes the very power of God.

Your spoken words activate the power of God within you. However, if you are afraid and don't have the faith to speak, the very power of God lies dormant.

Your Words Are Indicators of Your Heart

> *You brood of vipers, how can you, being evil, speak what is good? For the mouth speaks out of that which fills the heart.*
> **(Matthew 12:34)**

When you speak, you are drawing from that which fills your heart. Before you open your mouth, your heart must become filled.

> *And do not get drunk with wine, for that is dissipation, but be filled with the Spirit, speaking to one another in psalms and hymns and spiritual songs, singing and making melody with your heart to the Lord.*
>
> **(Ephesians 5:18-19)**

There are indicators that your heart is filled with the word of God. When you are filled with wine, your speech is unique to wine's inducement. When you are filled with the Spirit, your speech is unique to the Spirit's inducement. When wine is in your heart its indicators come out of your mouth. When the Spirit of God is in your heart, its indicators come out of your mouth.

When God engraves power potential in your heart, He expects you to utilize it. He doesn't expect you to ask Him to help you do what He has already enabled you to do.

> *But what does it say? "The word is near you, in your mouth and in your heart"—that is, the word of faith which we are preaching, that if you confess with your mouth Jesus as Lord, and believe in your heart that*

God raised Him from the dead, you will be saved; for with the heart a person believes, resulting in righteousness, and with the mouth he confesses, resulting in salvation. For the Scripture says, "Whoever believes in him will not be disappointed." For there is no distinction between Jew and Greek; for the same Lord is Lord of all, abounding in riches for all who call on Him; for "Whoever will call on the name of the lord will be saved."

How then will they call on Him in whom they have not believed? How will they believe in Him whom they have not heard? And how will they hear without a preacher? How will they preach unless they are sent? Just as it is written, "How beautiful are the feet of those who bring good news of good things!" However, they did not all heed the good news; for Isaiah says, "LORD, who has believed our report?" So faith comes from hearing, and hearing by the word of Christ.

(Romans 10:8-17)

Your faith comes by hearing the word of Christ, and you are to speak the word. For the word is in your mouth and heart. Therefore when you speak the word of Christ that is within your heart, it produces further faith. To hear is to take the word through your ear into your heart and out of your own mouth.

> *Therefore, let us fear if, while a promise remains of entering His rest, any one of you may seem to have come short of it. For indeed we have had good news preached to us, just as they also; but the word they heard did not profit them, because it was not united by faith in those who heard.*
> **(Hebrews 4:1-2)**

They heard with their ears, but the words they heard didn't the profit them. Why? Because the words they heard never ventured into their hearts.

God has never taken kindly to people who speak against His projects. That's why the Israelites died in the wilderness. They were foolish enough to speak against God. When God revealed to them His land promise project, the Israelites spoke contrarily.

They discouraged themselves by saying, *"We should have stayed in the land of Egypt."* After everything that God had done, they spoke against Him. Therefore, God said, "If I can't get you to declare that you can possess the land, I will not allow you to enter." The generation that mocked God perished in the wilderness after spending forty years wandering in it. That's awful! They were foolish enough to speak against God, and they died.

Refuse to engage in fearful conversation. When others attempt to engage you in fearful conversation, just walk away from them and leave them talking to themselves. Don't get yourself in trouble.

God grant me the wisdom to never speak against You and fall into spiritual danger. I will speak Your truths and live, even when others disagree.

CHAPTER FIVE

WHAT YOU SAY OVERRULES WHAT YOU INTEND

What You Say Overrules What You Intend

Cataracts dimmed Isaac's eyesight, as he grew old and drew nearer to the uncertain day of his death. As the day of his departure loomed ever closer, the need to pass on his patriarchal blessing to his oldest son, Esau, became more intense. So he called Esau, and asked him to prepare meal of fresh wild game and savory soup before passing on the blessing.

Isaac's treacherous wife, Rebekah, overheard the conversation between Isaac and Esau. Because she favored Esau's twin brother, Jacob, she concocted a deceitful scheme to steal the blessing for him. While

Esau hunted for game she had Jacob kill two goats and cook a savory dish for Isaac.

When Rebekah and Jacob had finished preparing the meal for Isaac, Jacob took it to his father. After Isaac had eaten, he blessed Jacob thinking that he was blessing his other son, Esau. The blessing of Jacob was for prosperity as well as for favor among his brothers (Genesis 27:1-29).

Shortly after Isaac blessed Jacob, Esau returned to receive his blessing. He and his father were surprised when they discovered that Jacob had intercepted his blessing through deceit. Esau's surprise quickly turned to murderous anger, which caused Rebekah to send Jacob away for his own safety. This deception caused a rift in their family that lasted for decades (Genesis 28:10-17).

Esau begged Isaac for another blessing. However, Isaac was unmoved by the deception of Jacob and the disappointment of Esau. *"Esau said to his father, 'Do you have only one blessing, my father? Bless me, even me also, O my father.' So Esau lifted his voice and wept"* **(Genesis 27:38)**.

The Power of the Spoken Word

With his spoken words, Isaac blessed his son Jacob. Isaac thought he was blessing Esau, but in reality it was Jacob. Furthermore, with his spoken words Isaac upheld the blessing of Jacob.

God seemed to have been with Jacob, even though he received his father's blessing by deception. In fact, God validated the blessing of Jacob.

> Then God appeared to Jacob again when he came from Paddan-aram, and He blessed him. God said to him, "Your name is Jacob; You shall no longer be called Jacob, But Israel shall be your name." Thus He called him Israel. God also said to him, "I am God Almighty; Be fruitful and multiply; A nation and a company of nations shall come from you, And kings shall come forth from you.
> **(Genesis 35:9-11)**

Isaac blessed his son, Jacob, with words that he spoke. His words set in motion the blessings that Jacob would later enjoy.
God Blessed Jacob, with words that He spoke. Even though Jacob had deceived his father, God upheld the spoken blessing.

Spoken Blessings Are Irrevocable

Here we see an important principle. First Isaac blessed Jacob, then God honored the blessing that Isaac spoke on his son. God Blessed Jacob because Isaac had blessed Jacob. What would have happened if Isaac had said nothing? God would have had nothing to honor. Even though Isaac blessed Jacob by mistake, God honored that spoken blessing.

Spoken blessings are irrevocable. Isaac declared, *"...Your brother came deceitfully and has taken away your blessing"* **(Genesis 27:35)**. Once words are spoken, they can't be taken back. You can never unsay what you've said. You can apologize, you can do whatever, but you can never unsay what you've said. So the blessing was in the power of Isaac's spoken words.

Genesis 27 records the blessing of the wrong son. Genesis 28 records the re-statement of the blessing.

What you say overrules what you intend. Therefore, you must consider carefully what you say before saying it...and never randomly repeat what someone else says.

The Angel of the Lord appeared to Moses and informed him of God's plans to deliver the children of Israel from Egyptian captivity.

Now Moses was pasturing the flock of Jethro his father-in-law, the priest of Midian; and he led the flock to the west side of the wilderness and came to Horeb, the mountain of God. The angel of the LORD appeared to him in a blazing fire from the midst of a bush..."

Therefore, come now, and I will send you to Pharaoh, so that you may bring My people, the sons of Israel, out of Egypt."

(Exodus 3:1-10)

God assigned Moses a central role in the deliverance of the Israelites.

As Moses led the Israelites toward the land of Canaan he became angry and allowed his attitude to interfere with his actions. *"They also provoked Him to wrath at the waters of Meribah, So that it went hard with Moses on their account; Because they were rebellious against His Spirit, He spoke rashly with his lips"*
(Psalms 106:32-33).

What you say overrules what you intend. You must verify what you say before saying it because it cannot be unsaid.

You can spend 30 years cultivating a good relationship and then allow a phrase to inadvertently fall from your lips and mess up everything. Inadvertent speaking caused Moses much agony. He had begun to accomplish one of the most gigantic tasks God had ever assigned one man. For all practical purposes, he had been successful.

Nevertheless, some will argue, *"Doesn't God know my heart?"* Yes, God knows your heart. You know your heart, too. Your heart is known by the words of your mouth, *for out of the abundance of the heart the mouth speaks* (see Matt. 12:34). What you say comes straight out of your heart.

God knows your heart, and He knows that your heart has a habit of saying things before you verify them. See, if you're in the habit of saying stuff before you verify it, how can it be in your heart to only say that which is true? It can't be. What's in your heart is the habit of saying whatever has come or been presented to you.

Prayerfully choose your words carefully. Before you say anything, even in your casual conversations, think about what you are going to say.

It is in You, Oh Lord that I ask for clarity in what I say. Fill my heart full of what Your word, the Bible, speaks so that my mouth will overflow with blessings.

CHAPTER SIX

THE GOD OF MY TONGUE

THE GOD OF MY TONGUE

God's mode of operation demands our attention.

Moses spoke the word of God, words that God Himself put in his mouth. *"Now then go, and I, even I, will be with your mouth, and teach you what you are to say"* **(Exodus 4:12)**.

In order for God to put his words into Moses' mouth, He had to first put his words into Moses spirit (heart) in abundance. Remember, out of the abundance of the heart the mouth speaks **(Matthew 12:34, Luke 6:45)**.

Moses didn't serve as a parrot for God. Moses became convinced within his own spirit, and then he spoke from that which filled his spirit.

Aaron spoke the word of Moses because Moses put his words into Aaron's mouth.

> *Then the anger of the LORD burned against Moses, and He said, "Is there not your brother Aaron the Levite? I know that he speaks fluently. And moreover, behold, he is coming out to meet you; when he sees you, he will be glad in his heart. You are to speak to him and put the words in his mouth; and I, even I, will be with your mouth and his mouth, and I will teach you what you are to do. Moreover, he shall speak for you to the people; and he will be as a mouth for you and you will be as God to him."*
>
> **(Exodus 4:14-16)**

In order for Moses to put his words into Aaron's mouth, he had to first put his words into Aaron's spirit (heart) in abundance. Again, out of the abundance of the heart the mouth speaks **(Matthew 12:34, Luke 6:45)**.

Likewise, Aaron didn't serve as a parrot for Moses. He first became convinced within his own spirit, and then spoke from that which filled his spirit.

Moses filled Aaron's heart with his word. Moses became as God to Aaron.

When someone fills your heart with his/her word, they become as God to you. Your parents

God's mode of operation demands our attention.

were as God to you during your childhood formative years. Even others who exercise dominant persuasive appeal are as God to you. *"Then the Lord said to Moses, See, I make you as God to Pharaoh, and your brother Aaron shall be your prophet"* **(Exodus 7:1).**

When you fill someone's heart with your word, you become as a God to them. God's mode of operation demands your attention.

Come everyone and clap for joy! Shout unto God, for the Lord God is above all gods and is awesome beyond words, hallelujah!

7

THE TONGUE OF MY GOD

THE TONGUE OF MY GOD

The Shunammite woman blessed the prophet Elisha, and then provided a place in her home for him to rest and be refreshed. In turn the prophet Elisha blessed the Shunammite woman, he prophesied a son for her by the mighty power of God.

Spoken words activated both her blessing for Elisha and his blessing for her. Both blessings resulted from the spoken word.

Now there came a day when Elisha passed over to Shunem, where there was a prominent woman, and she persuaded him to eat food. And so it was, as often as he passed by, he turned in there to eat food. She said to her husband, "Behold now, I perceive that this is a holy man of God passing by us continually. "Please, let us make a little walled upper chamber and let us set a bed for him there, and a table and a chair and a lampstand; and it shall be, when he comes to us, that he can turn in there."

One day he came there and turned in to the upper chamber and rested. Then he said to Gehazi his servant, "Call this Shunammite." And when he had called her, she stood before him. He said to him, "Say now to her, 'Behold, you have been careful for us with all this care; what can I do for you? Would you be spoken for to the king or to the captain of the army?'" And she answered, "I live among my own people." So he said, "What then is to be done for her?" And Gehazi answered, "Truly she has no son and her husband is old." He said, "Call her." When he had called her, she stood in the doorway. Then he said, "At this season next year you will embrace a son." And she said,

"No, my lord, O man of God, do not lie to your maidservant."

The woman conceived and bore a son at that season the next year, as Elisha had said to her.

(2 Kings 4:8-17)

Despite her being given to hospitality, she experienced a great heartache. Her son died.

When the child was grown, the day came that he went out to his father to the reapers. He said to his father, "My head, my head." And he said to his servant, "Carry him to his mother." When he had taken him and brought him to his mother, he sat on her lap until noon, and then died.

(2 Kings 4:18-20)

However, her heartache was turned to happiness as Elisha returned her son to her alive.

When Elisha came into the house, behold the lad was dead and laid on his bed. So he entered and shut the door behind them both and prayed to the Lord. And he went up and lay on the child, and put his

mouth on his mouth and his eyes on his eyes and his hands on his hands, and he stretched himself on him; and the flesh of the child became warm. Then he returned and walked in the house once back and forth, and went up and stretched himself on him; and the lad sneezed seven times and the lad opened his eyes. He called Gehazi and said, "Call this Shunammite." So he called her. And when she came in to him, he said, "Take up your son." Then she went in and fell at his feet and bowed herself to the ground, and she took up her son and went out.
(2 Kings 4:32-37)

Because she spoke a word of faith in the midst of her grief, her heartache was turned to happiness. Imagine the joy she experienced during the years given by the new lease on life of her son.

She went up and laid him on the bed of the man of God, and shut the door behind him and went out. Then she called to her husband and said, "Please send me one of the servants and one of the don-

keys that I may run to the man of God and return." He said, "Why will you go to him today? It is neither a new moon nor Sabbath." And she said, "It will be well." Then she saddled a donkey and said to her servant, "Drive and go forward; do not slow down the pace for me unless I tell you." So she went and came to the man of God to Mount Carmel. When the man of God saw her at a distance, he said to Gehazi his servant, "Behold, there is the Shunammite. Please run now to meet her and say to her, 'Is it well with you? Is it well with your husband? Is it well with the child?'" And she answered, "It is well."

(2 Kings 4:21-26)

[By faith] Women received back their dead by resurrection; and others were tortured, not accepting their release, so that they might obtain a better resurrection.

(Hebrews 11:35)

The spoken words of the Shunammite woman programmed her life for life. Her spoken words provide for the blessing of Elisha, which in turn nurtured his blessing to her.

Your faith-filled spoken words program your life for life.

Your faith-filled spoken words add value to the lives of those who *know* you. You have a "faith" story to show and you ought to show your story. The Shunammite woman's faith-filled spoken words added value to the life of her son. Also, her faith-filled spoken words added value to the life of her husband.

Your faith-filled spoken words add value to the lives of those who *hear* of you. You have a "faith" story to tell and you ought to tell your story. Her faith-filled words added value to the life of those of her generation who heard about her demonstration of faith. Even now, her faith-filled spoken words add value to the lives of those of this generation who hear this story **(Hebrews 11:4).**

It never has to be over until God says it is over. Sometimes God says that it is over only because we

> Your faith-filled spoken words add value to the lives of those who *know* and *hear* you. You have a "faith" story and you ought to show and tell your story.

say that it is over. He never told Moses to stop negotiating for the salvation of Sodom and Gomorrah **(Genesis 18:32-33)**. No doubt, he could have saved the city on the basis of one righteous person, the righteousness of himself. Lest you think that is far fetched, Jesus Christ, on the basis of one righteous person, can save the entire world. God wants you to speak hopefully until after He has absolutely indicated that He has written the final chapter.

Yes, Lord because I want a long good life, then I will watch my tongue! I will keep my lips from evil and spend my time pursuing peace, Amen.

CHAPTER EIGHT

MY SPOKEN WORDS FUNCTION ACCORDING TO SPIRITUAL LAW

My Spoken Words Function According To Spiritual Law

Christianity is more than mere rules and formulas. Christianity is a life-style. It is a complex but not complicated process designed to lead you to the fullness of Christ. *"Until we all attain to the unity of the faith, and of the knowledge of the Son of God, to a mature man, to the measure of the stature which belongs to the fullness of Christ"* **(Ephesians 4:13).**

Therefore, Christianity involves a dynamic interaction between God, Christ, and man. *"So then, my beloved, just as you have always obeyed, not as in my presence only, but now much more in my absence, work out your salvation with fear and trembling; for it is God who is at work in you, both to will and to work for His good pleasure"* **(Philippians 2:12-13).**

People have often asked, *"Why do bad things happen to good people"?* But this question needs to be answered as well: *"Why do good things happen to bad people"?*

God created the natural laws of sowing and reaping. Likewise, He created a spiritual law of sowing and reaping. *"Now this I say, he who sows sparingly will also reap sparingly, and he who sows bountifully will also reap bountifully"* **(2 Corinthians 9:6).**

> *"Do not be deceived, God is not mocked; for whatever a man sows, this he will also reap. For the one who sows to his own flesh will from the flesh reap corruption, but the one who sows to the Spirit will from the Spirit reap eternal life. Let us not lose heart in doing good, for in due time we will reap if we do not grow weary."*
>
> **(Galatians 6:7-9)**

According To God's Laws

By no means can we explain every thing that happens. But, we can understand great probabilities. Many of your ills in life come because you fail to respect universal laws.

Gravity functions according to natural law. If bad people (whomever you deem to be bad) intentionally honor the law of gravity what happens? Pleasurable experiences will likely follow.

If bad people ignorantly honor the law of gravity what happens? Once again, pleasurable experiences will likely follow. Whether bad people honor intentionally or ignorantly, God does not withhold pleasurable experiences from them.

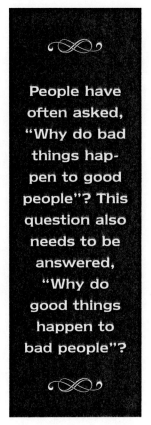

People have often asked, "Why do bad things happen to good people"? This question also needs to be answered, "Why do good things happen to bad people"?

If good people (whomever you deem to be good) dishonor the law of gravity willingly what happens? Painful experiences will likely follow.

If good people dishonor the law of gravity ignorantly what happens? Painful experiences will likely follow. Whether good people dishonor willingly or ignorantly, God does not withhold painful experiences from them.

The spoken word functions according to spiritual law. If bad people honor the law of the spoken word intentionally, what happens? Pleasurable experiences will likely follow.

If bad people honor the law of the spoken word ignorantly what happens? Pleasurable experiences will likely follow. Whether they honor intentionally or ignorantly, God does not withhold pleasurable experiences from them **(Matthew 8:5-10)**.

If good people dishonor the law of the spoken word intentionally what happens? Painful experiences will likely follow.

If good people dishonor the law of the spoken word ignorantly what happens? Painful experiences will likely follow.

Whether they dishonor intentionally or ignorantly, God does not withhold painful experiences from them **(Numbers 20:6-13; Psalms 106:33; 2 Samuel 6:3-10; Numbers 4:1-15; 7:9)**.

Most people have no problem when bad folk do dishonorable things and endure the painful consequences of their behavior. Nor do they have a problem when good people do honorable things and enjoy the pleasurable consequences of their behavior. But some take issue when bad people enjoy pleasurable consequences. These same folk have a problem when good people endure painful consequences.

God allows it to rain on the just and unjust. God allows the warm glow of His love to rain on the just and unjust. Thank you Lord!

CHAPTER NINE

I MUST SAY
WHAT THE
WORD SAYS

T I Must Say What the Word Says

The angel Gabriel informed Mary that God had chosen her to give birth to His Son, Jesus.

Now in the sixth month the angel Gabriel was sent from God to a city in Galilee called Nazareth, to a virgin engaged to a man whose name was Joseph, of the descendants of David; and the virgin's name was Mary. And coming in, he said to her, "Greetings, favored one! The Lord is with you." But she was very perplexed at this statement, and kept pondering what kind of salutation this was. The angel said to her, "Do not be afraid, Mary; for you have found favor with God. And behold, you will conceive in your womb and bear a son, and you shall name Him Jesus. He will be great and will be called the Son of the Most High; and the Lord God will give Him the throne of His father David; and He will reign over the house of Jacob forever, and His kingdom will have no end." Mary said to the angel, "How can this be, since I am a virgin?" The angel answered and said to her, "The Holy Spirit will come upon you, and the power of the Most High will overshadow you; and for that reason the holy Child shall be called the Son of God."

(Luke 1:26-35)

Mary had no knowledge of a virgin ever giving birth to a child. Therefore, she questioned the angel as to how she could. Despite the seemingly impossible, she believed what God had said about her. *"And Mary said, 'Behold, the bond slave of the Lord; may it be done to me according to your word.' And the angel departed from her"* **(Luke 1:38)**. Like Mary, you must condition yourself to believe what the word says.

Say What The Word Says

Mary began to say what the word said, even before it happened. "And Mary said, 'My soul exalts the Lord, and my spirit has rejoiced in God my Savior…' For He has had regard for the humble state of His bond slave; for behold, from this time on all generations will count me blessed" **(Luke 1:46-48)**. What she said became a reality when she gave birth to Jesus. Her words became a creative force within her.

Surround yourself with people who will say what the word says. Mary visited Elizabeth, the soon-to-be mother of John the Baptist (Luke 1:39-44). Elizabeth knew that Mary was to give birth to a child. How did Elizabeth know that Mary was going to give birth? **(Luke 1:41,45)** She believed the word that Mary had heard.

You must condition yourself to believe what the word says. God wants you to begin speaking about yourself what the word says about you. *"What does the word say about me?"* is a very important question for you to answer.

The word says that if you are in Christ you are a new creature. *"Therefore if anyone is in Christ, he is a new creature; the old things passed away; behold, new things have come"* **(2 Cor. 5:17)**.

DECLARE YOUR DESTINY – UNLEASH THE POWER OF SPOKEN WORDS

How did that happen?

God reconciled (reestablished a favorable relationship with) those who are in Christ. *"Now all these things are from God, who reconciled us to Himself through Christ and gave us the ministry of reconciliation"* **(2 Cor. 5:18)**.

How did that happen?

God canceled your sin debt. *"Namely, that God was in Christ reconciling the world to Himself, not counting their trespasses against them, and He has committed to us the word of reconciliation"* **(2 Cor. 5:19)**.

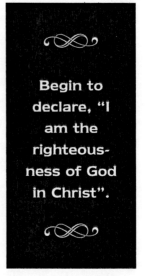

Begin to declare, "I am the righteousness of God in Christ".

How did that happen?

God made Christ to be sin for you. *"He made Him who knew no sin to be sin on our behalf, so that we might become the righteousness of God in Him"* **(2 Cor. 5:21)**.

Therefore, you are the righteousness of God. You are not just a poor old sinner. Begin to say, *"I am the righteousness of God in Christ!"*

Father because You said who I was before I knew who I was, I now declare that I am the righteousness of You in Christ. Make me know more of whom I am.

10

CHAPTER TEN

I CAN SPEAK MY PROBLEM AWAY

I Can Speak My Problem Away

God created words as a power force within the universe. Using the word of his power, He spoke things into existence **(Genesis 1:3)**. Through the word of his power, God maintains the existence of that which he created and desires to exist **(Hebrews 1:3)**.

God's mode of operation demands your attention. You must condition yourself to believe the word. Your faith-filled spoken words program your life for life.

Your spoken words are a most powerful force within the universe. Your spoken words are powerful enough to create a curse **(Mark 11:12-14, 20-21)**, and your spoken words are powerful enough to create a blessing **(Mark 11:23-24)**.

When you exercise faith, your faith-filled words can improve the circumstances of life. You exercise your faith in God by speaking to the problem. Jesus taught his disciples to speak to their problems.

> *And Jesus answered saying to them, "Have faith in God. Truly I say to you, whoever says to this mountain, 'Be taken up and cast into the sea,' and does not doubt in his heart, but believes that what he says is going to happen, it will be granted him."*
>
> **(Mark 11:22-23)**

You exercise your faith in God by speaking the solution to the problem. Jesus taught the disciples to speak what they wanted done—"be taken up and cast into the sea." Don't just state the problem, but state the solution as well.

It's important not to deny the existence of the problem. But, do deny the right of the problem to exist. For example, don't deny that people steal, but do deny their right to steal. Don't deny that unfairness exists within the work place, but do deny the right of unfairness to exist within the workplace.

When you deny something's right to exist, you exercise your right to ask it to leave.

Jesus did not teach his disciples to deny that the mountain existed. He taught them to believe and demand that it would be there no longer. *"Therefore I say to you, all things for which you pray and ask, believe that you have received them, and they will be granted you"* **(Mark 11:24).**

Peter did not deny that the man in Acts 3:1 was lame—he had been lame since birth, more than forty years **(Acts 3:2; 4:22)**. However, Peter did deny the right for paralysis to exist any longer within the man's body **(Acts 3:6)**. Therefore, the lame man was healed.

Expect Things To Get Better

Expect circumstances to improve. Jesus taught that when you have faith in God, you could ask circumstances to change. He taught that what you said and believed you could have **(Mark 11:24)**.

If you have faith in God but say and believe that circumstances will get worse, you will have what you say. People who say "it will get worse" and it gets worse, may see themselves as prophetic. They are not prophetic but pathetic for they have spoken a curse into their life.

Lord, I will consciously labor to direct the way of my thoughts that will train my tongue to speak the wonderful blessings of Your word.

ABOUT THE AUTHOR

John Marshall is an author, counselor, editor, executive media producer, facilitator for conflict resolution, motivational speaker, office manager, preacher, public relations director, teacher, trainer, relationship consultant and writer.

He studied at Freed-Hardeman and Southern Christian Universities, as well as the University of Memphis.

He also hosts "Call & Ask", a national telecast, and has taught in 94 cities, 16 states, and 1 foreign country.

TAPE SERIES BY JOHN MARSHALL

Powerful Life Changing Teaching Tape Series

Each album contains six audio cassettes @ $29.99

CHURCH DEVELOPMENT

CDUST   ***"Shake the Dust***
Objective: To help you travel the difficult roads of disagreement within the church.

CPLDG   ***"I Pledge My Allegiance"***
Objective: To help you to properly salute God.

FAMILY DEVELOPMENT

FHHWW   ***"Help for Husbands/A Word to Wives"***
Objective: To help husbands and wives understandably relate to each other.

FMYTH **"Myths That Make Life Miserable"**
Objective: To help you become aware of the myths that steal the joy of marriage.

FVISN **"God's Vision for the Family"**
Objective: To help you to activate God's vision for yourself and your family.

PERSONAL DEVELOPMENT

PDPRS **"Shortening Your Session with Depression"**
Objective: To help you to minimize the impact of depression.

PHBTS **"Breaking Bad Habits"**
Objective: To help you to embrace principles that lead to the breaking of bad habits.

PPTNT **"Reaching Your Maximum Potential"**
Objective: to help you to set your heart and become what you have set your heart

PSCSS **"Success In All Of Life"**
Objective: To help you to experience the fellowship between sacrifice and success.

PTONG **"The Power of the Tongue"**
Objective: To help you to change your world by changing your words.

PWRRY **"Kick the Habit of Worry"**
Objective: To help you stop worry

SPIRITUAL DEVELOPMENT

SESVD **"Eternally Saved and Secured"**
Objective: To help you to know that your salvation is secure.

SPRAY *"Teach Us to Pray"*
Objective: To help you to understandably pray spiritually enriched prayers.

SSPRT *"Listen! Your Spirit is Speaking"*
Objective: To help you learn to listen to your spirit thereby renewing your mind.

To order or learn more about John Marshall Ministries:
Call (404) 286-1139
Email: JM@JohnMarshallMinistries.Net
Visit: www.JohnMarshallMinistries.Net